# WORDS IN COLOR

# INSPIRING POETRY, ORIGINAL ARTWORK AND A COLORING BOOK.

## BY DARRELL MITCHELL

DM INK PUBLISHING

# COPYRIGHT

# DEDICATION

*I dedicate this book to my kids, Macayla, Siara, Mavi'e, & Maceo.*

# TABLE OF CONTENTS

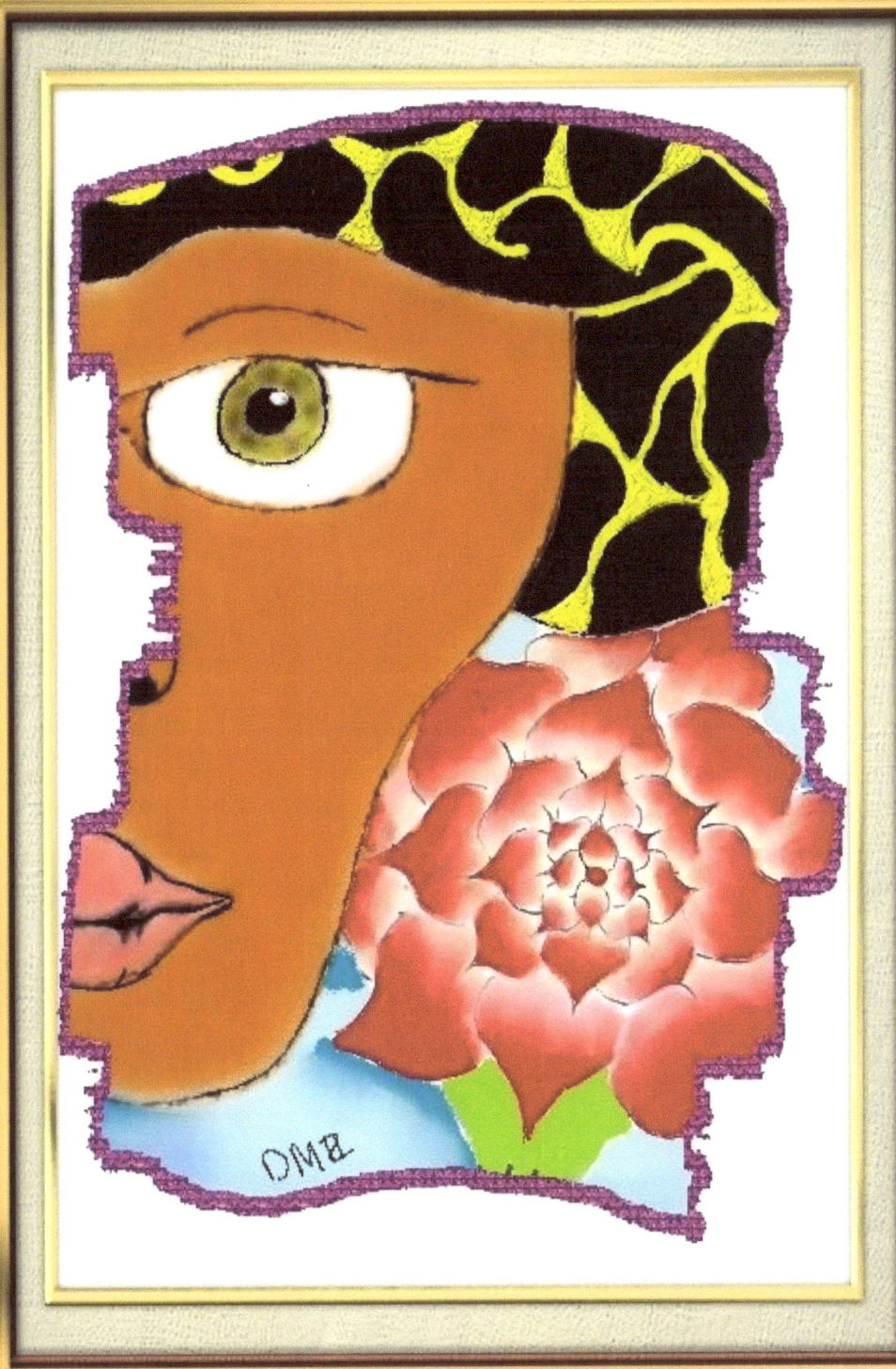

1

LADY ROSE

Everlasting Love


As subtle as a whisper and as clear as a microscope

You saw through my mess

And found a deep buried seed of hope

The hope to love

The hope to trust

The hope to be led

From a place that I was so comfortable in.

My heart kept telling me to let you in no matter

How much I wanted to give up,

I gave in, and

When I did it was magical

The greatest achievement I ever made in my life was overcoming the

fear to love you

And though this is new to me.

The divine reality is in theory here we stand, the man and his rib.

And in our garden we have the love of our kids, our friends,

Our family, And when it rains it rains blessings

On us, and as we grow in love &

In trust, God will lead us in this every lasting

Love.

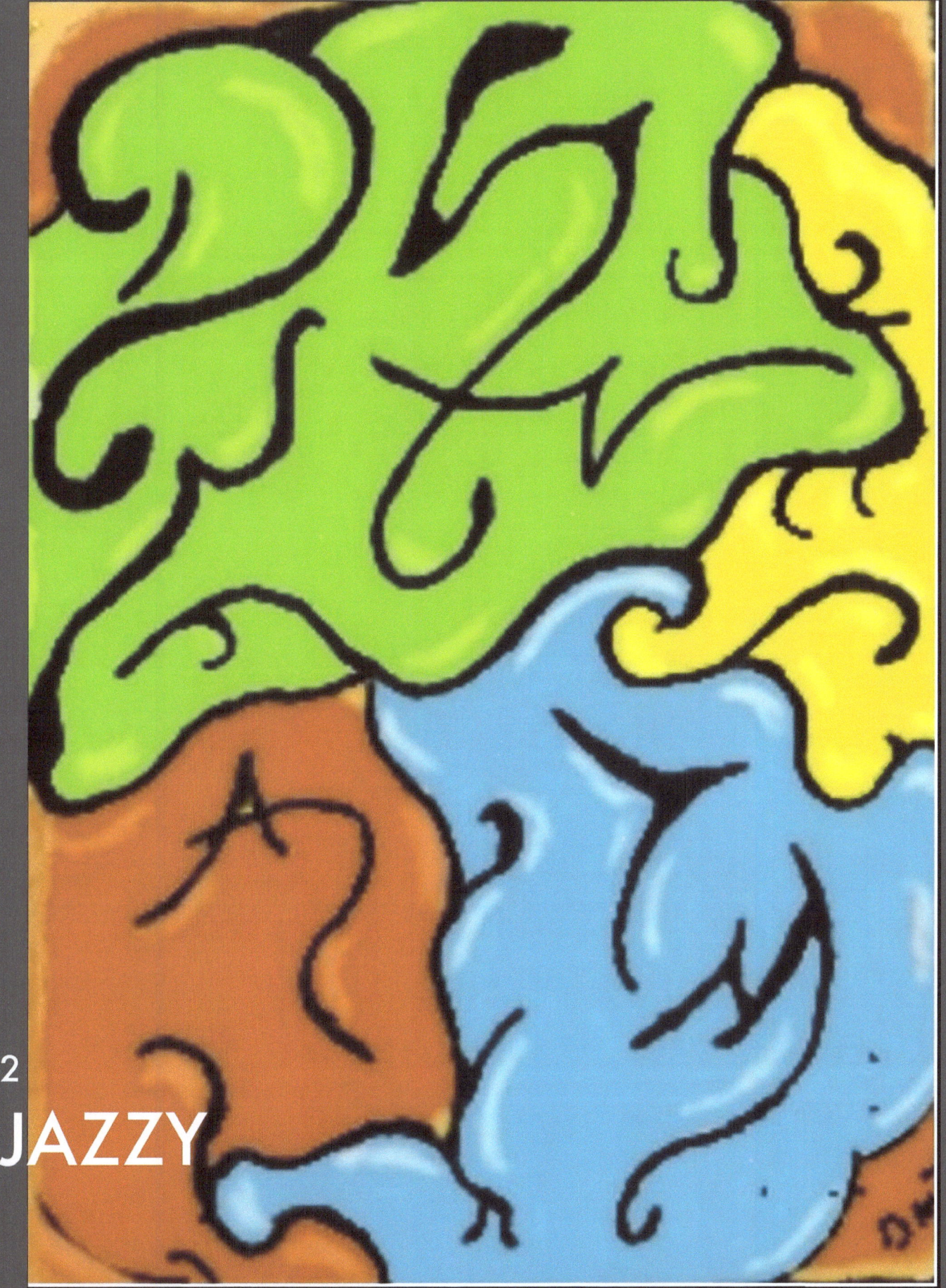

2

JAZZY

# CHOICES

BLACK CROWS REMIND ME OF
UNIQUE PROSE,
SO I CHOOSE TRUTH OVER HAIKU,
FACTS FORMATTING LIKE MAPS,
BRIDGING THE GENERATIONAL
GAP BETWEEN THE ELDERLY
AND THE YOUTH.
SO GOD CHANGED MY NAME
AFTER I CHOOSE PURPOSE OVER
FAME,
NOW I REPRESENT THE
KINGDOM WITH RIGHTEOUSNESS
INSTEAD OF BEING ENGRAVED
WITH SHAME.

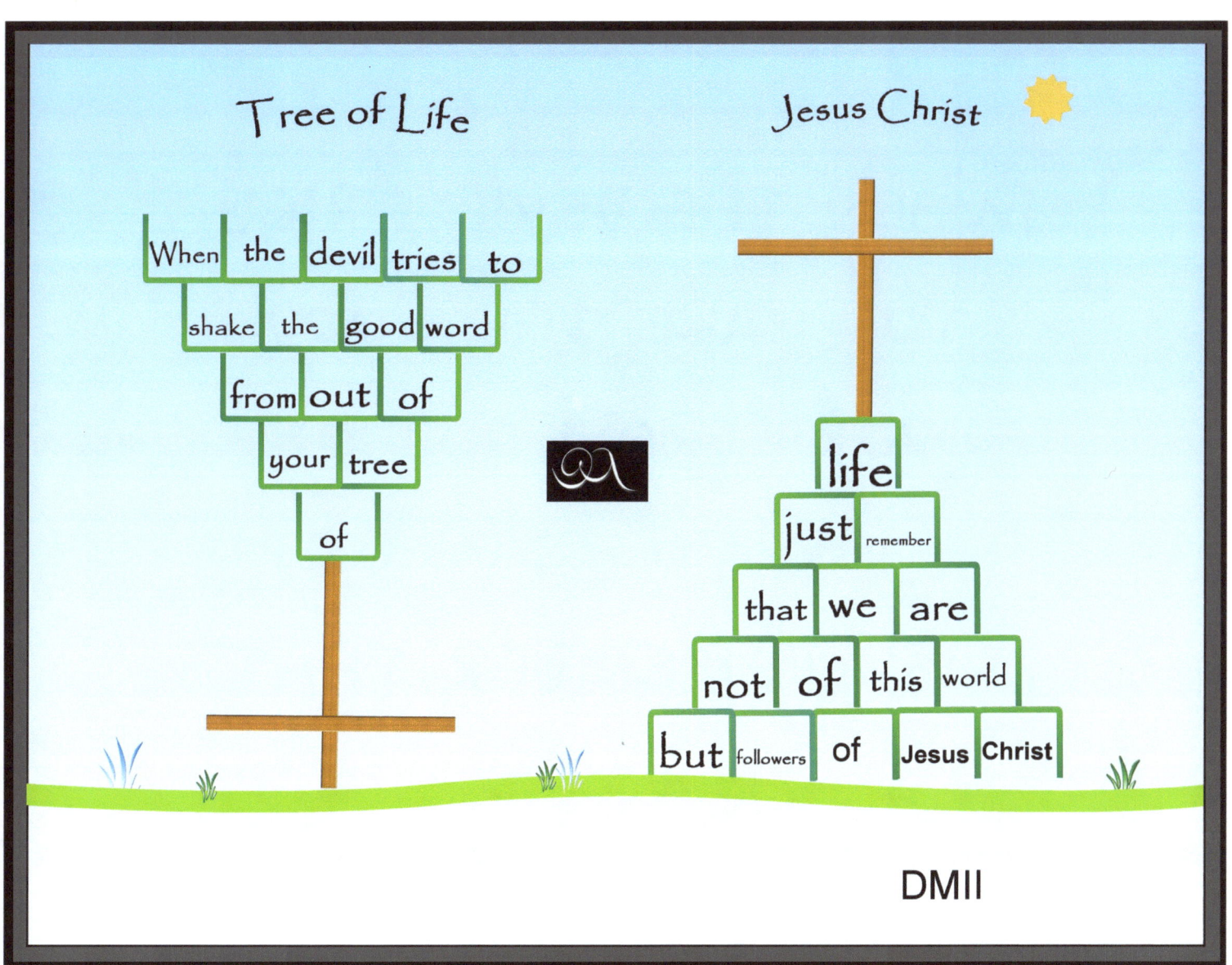

3

# TREE OF LIFE

# TREE OF LIFE POEM

WHEN THE DEVIL TRIES
TO SHAKE THE GOOD
WORD FROM OUT OF
YOUR TREE OF LIFE.
JUST REMEMBER THAT
WE ARE NOT OF THIS
WORLD BUT
FOLLOWERS OF JESUS
CHRIST.

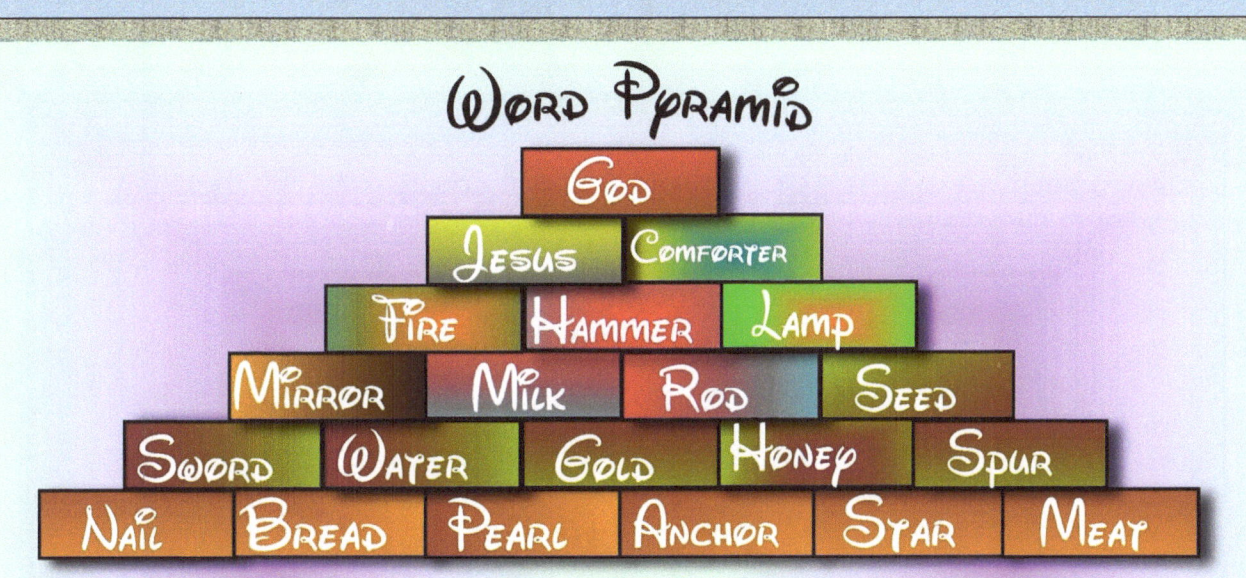

Word Pyramid

GOD

JESUS — COMFORTER

FIRE — HAMMER — LAMP

MIRROR — MILK — ROD — SEED

SWORD — WATER — GOLD — HONEY — SPUR

NAIL — BREAD — PEARL — ANCHOR — STAR — MEAT

Reading can get you knowledge, if you have not heard, And if knowledge is power, then there is power in words
Words can be like meat, strenght giving and good to eat, Like a mirror it reveals who we are and desire to be
Like a star it guides at night, Like a anchor it can hold you down in a storm
Like a fire it burns, cleanses, and keeps you warm, It's like a pearl, a precious gem
Like bread it keeps us fed, Like honey it leaves a sweet taste
Like a nail it can set things in a sure place, It's like gold or a priceless treasure
Like water it's life giving, a seed producing life, Like milk it's nourishing
It's like a sharp double edged sword, Its like a rod or a measuring instrument
Like a spur it pricks my conscience, Like a hammer it smashes and demolishes
Its a lamp an instrument of light in the dark, like a comforter never leaving our hearts alone
like a savior it represents for the entire human race, Powerful as if God left words on earth in his place.

Poem & Picture by Darrell Mitchell II

DM Ink Publishing

Think.Write.Life

4

# WORD PYRAMID

# WORD PYRAMID

Reading can help you acquire knowledge, if you haven't heard,

and if knowledge is power,

then there's power in words.

Words can be like **meat**, strength-giving and good to eat

Like a **mirror**, it reveals to us what we are and what we can be,

Like a **star**, it guides

like an **anchor** it can hold you down in a storm

Like a **fire** it burns, cleanses you and keeps you warm

It's like a **pearl**, a precious gem,

like bread, it keeps us fed

Like a nail it can set things in a sure place

Like honey, it can leave a sweet taste

It's like gold or priceless treasures

and it's like water, life giving & refreshing

It's like a seed producing life

Like milk it's nourishing

Like a sharp sword it's piercing,

it can be a rod or a measuring instrument

Like a spur pricking my conscience,

it's like a hammer as it smashes and demolishes

it's like a lamp an instrument of light in the dark.

it's like a **comforter** in our memories, never leaving our hearts alone

it's like a **savior** as it represents for the entire human race

Words are so powerful it's as if **God** left words on earth in his place.

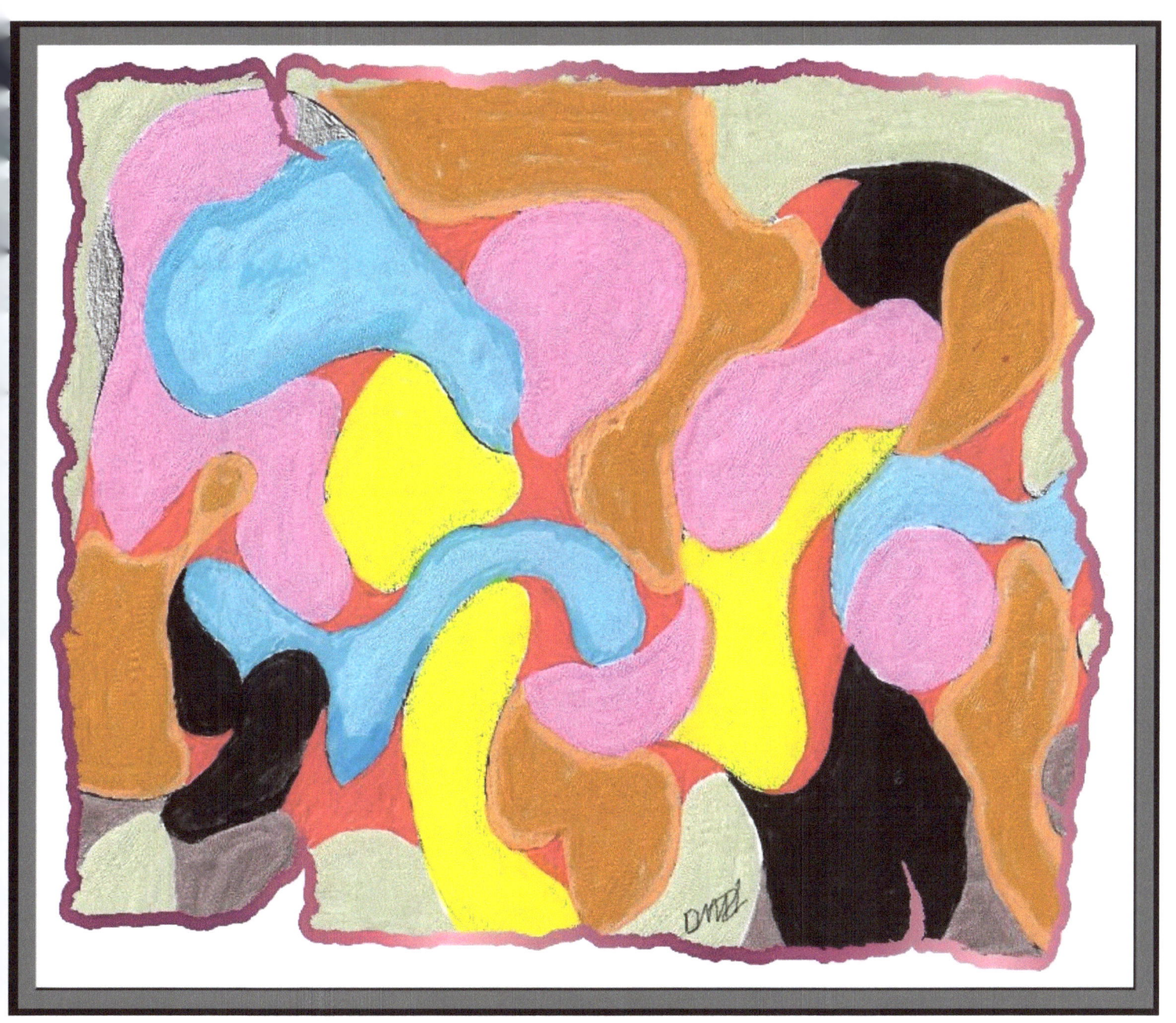

5

# ABSTRACT

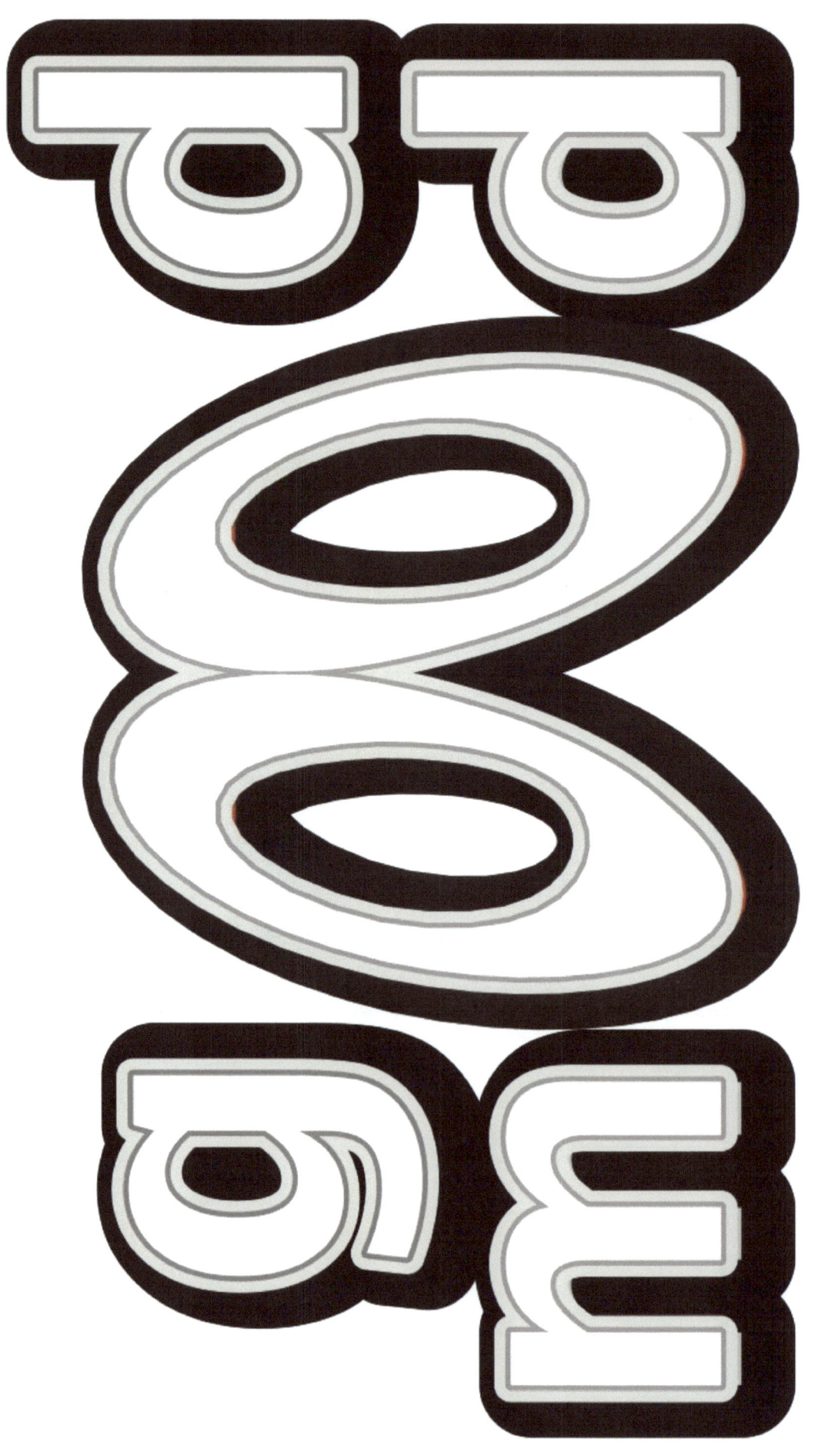

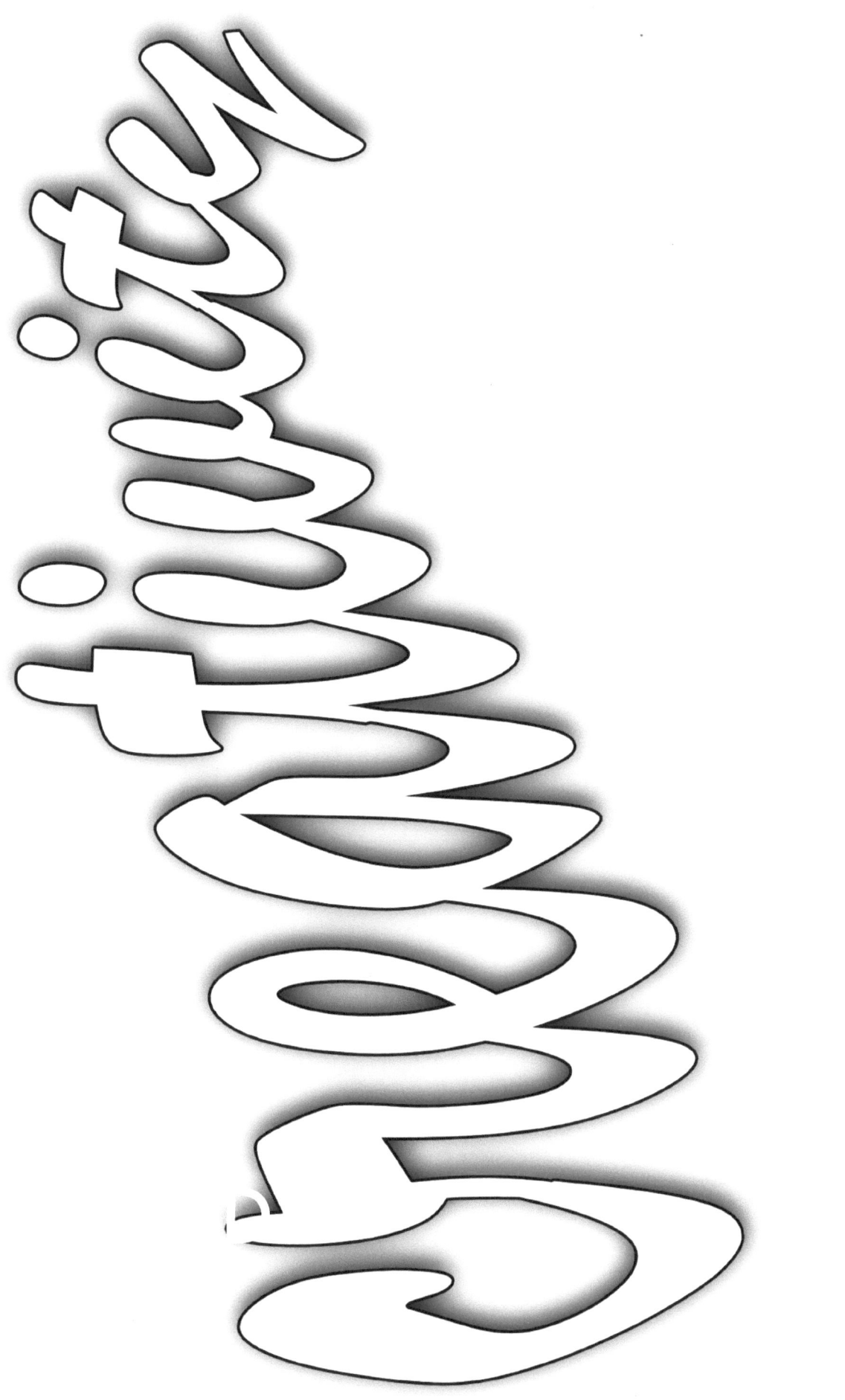

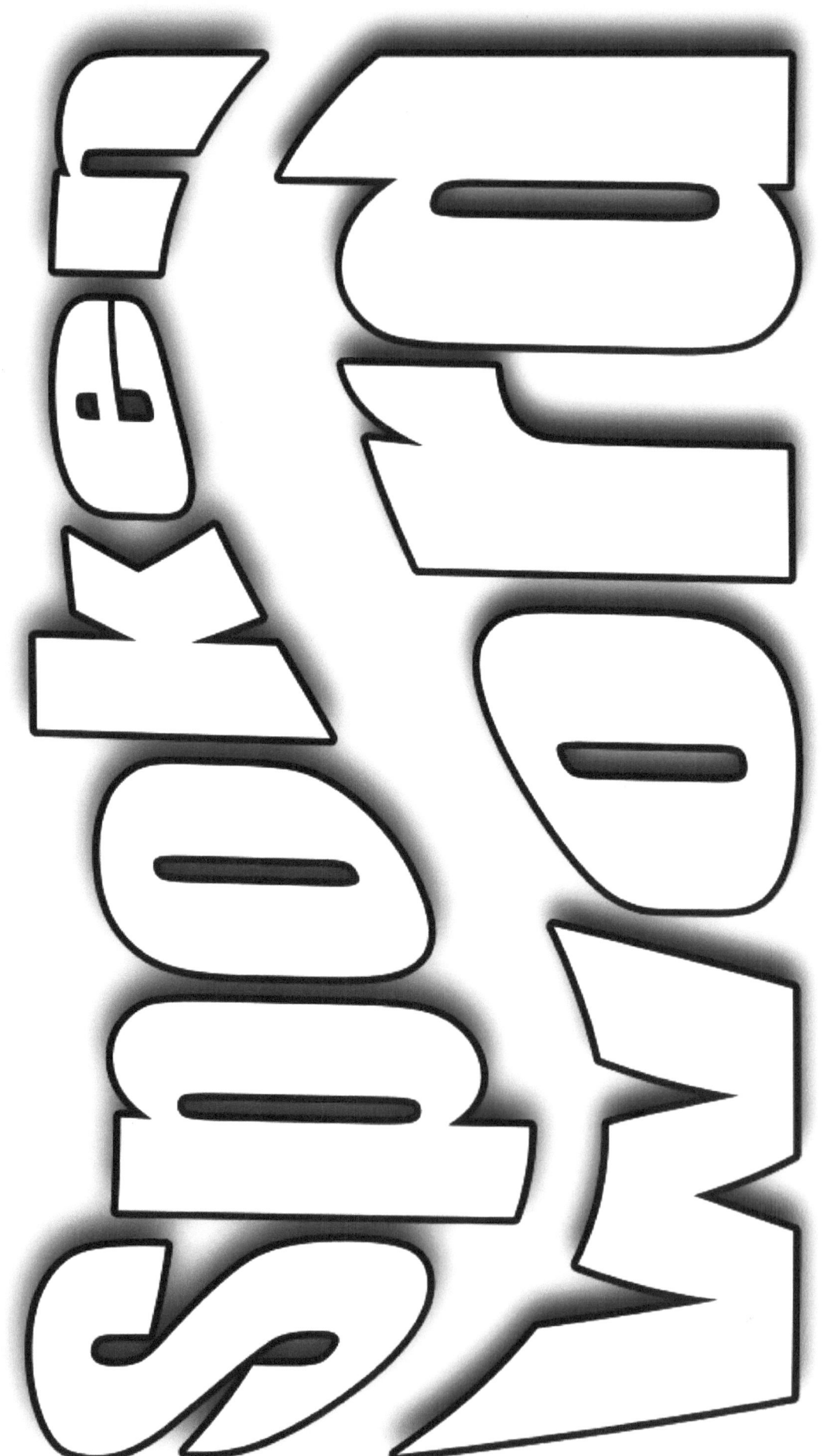

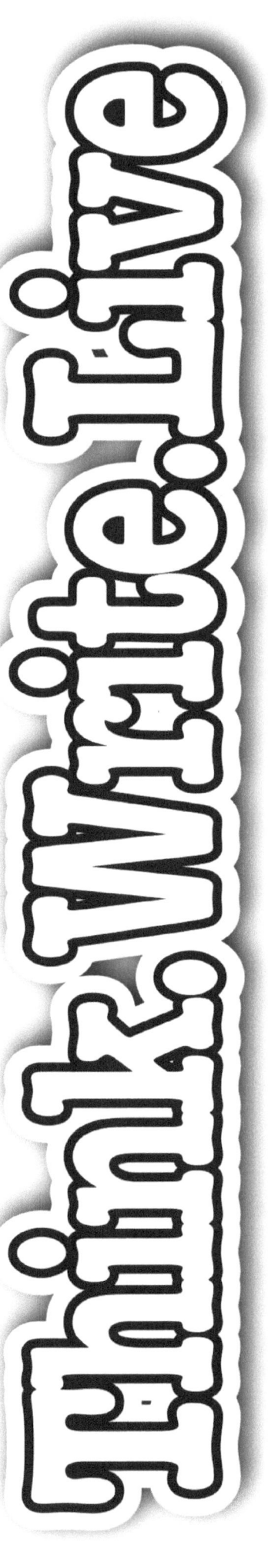

Think. Write. Live.

Be Inspired

# About The Author

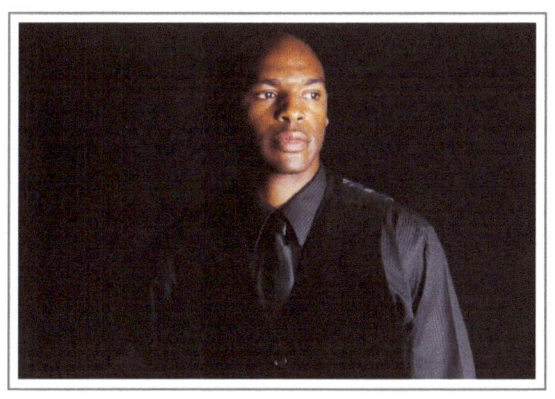

The Los Angeles, Ca based Author, Poet, Publisher and Artist has been performing spoken word poetry for the last decade and has competed in and hosted various poetry slams, cruises, open mic events, locally and internationally. The writer has also been featured in articles spotlighting performances from features, theatre plays, community outreach projects, performing arts programs and workshops.

The Author currently has Poetry books, compact disk, Artwork and Performance videos that have gone viral and are currently viewed numerous times a day through national and international channels.

The poetic stories have been described as inspirational, powerful and family friendly, most importantly it address everyday aspects of life and offers a different perspective. Through his work Darrell has moved generations, influenced ideas and empowered readers and listeners to enjoy life and achieve their dreams.